INSECTS 2

Published by Creative Education, 123 South Broad Street, Mankato, Minnesota 56001

Printed by permission of Wildlife Education, Ltd.

ISBN 0-88682-776-0

INSECTS 2

Creative Education

Art Credits

All paintings by Walter Stuart

Photographic Credits

Front Cover: Wayne Lynch (*DRK Photo*)

Page Six: Peter Ward (*Bruce Coleman, Inc.*)

Page Eight: Top Left, Kim Taylor (*Bruce Coleman, Ltd.*); **Top Right, Stephen Dalton** (*Photo Researchers*); **Bottom Right,** Jeff March (*Tom Stack & Associates*)

Page Nine: Top, Kjell B. Sandved; **Bottom,** J.L. Mason (*Ardea London*)

Page Ten: Top, Pietrzyk (*Tom Stack & Associates*); **Middle Left,** Kjell B. Sandved; **Middle Right,** J.L.G. Grande (*Bruce Coleman, Inc.*); **Bottom,** P. Morris (*Ardea London*)

Page Eleven: Top, Shostal Associates; **Middle Left,** Ray Simons (*Photo Researchers*); **Middle Right and Bottom,** P.H. Ward (*Natural Science Photos*)

Page Twelve: Top, Middle, and Bottom Right, Kjell B. Sandved; **Bottom Left,** Manfred Kage (*Peter Arnold, Inc.*)

Page Thirteen: Top Left, Anthony Bannister (*Natural History Photographic Agency*); **Top Right,** Kjell B. Sandved; **Middle,** Thomas Eisner; **Bottom Left,** E.R. Degginger (*Bruce Coleman, Inc.*); **Bottom Right,** Kjell B. Sandved

Pages Fourteen and Fifteen: Preston-Mafham (*Animals Animals*)

Page Sixteen: Top, A. Kerstitch (*Tom Stack & Associates*); **Middle,** Terry Domico (*West Stock*); **Bottom,** Michael Ederegger (*DRK Photo*)

Page Seventeen: Top, Terry Domico (*Earth Images*); **Bottom,** Lynn M. Stone (*Bruce Coleman, Inc.*)

Page Eighteen: Top, Donald Specker (*Animals Animals*); **Middle,** M.P.L. Fogden (*Bruce Coleman, Ltd.*); **Bottom Left,** Root (*Okapia*); **Bottom Right,** Michael Ederegger (*Peter Arnold, Inc.*)

Page Nineteen: Top, Stephen Dalton (*Photo Researchers*); **Middle Left,** Oxford Scientific Films/Animals Animals; **Middle Right,** Stephen Dalton (*Photo Researchers*); **Middle,** Hans Pfletschinger (*Peter Arnold, Inc.*); **Bottom Left,** Terry Domico (*Earth Images*); **Bottom Right,** Hans Pfletschinger (*Peter Arnold, Inc.*)

Page Twenty: Top Left, Middle Left and Bottom Left, Kjell B. Sandved; **Top Right,** Dwight Kuhn (*Bruce Coleman, Ltd.*); **Middle Right,** Mik Dakin (*Bruce Coleman, Ltd.*); **Bottom Right,** Terry Domico (*Earth Images*)

Page Twenty-One: Top, Alan Root (*Survival Anglia*); **Middle Left,** Stephen J. Krasemann (*DRK Photo*); **Middle Right,** V.E. Ward (*Photo Researchers*); **Bottom Left,** Robert Carr (*Bruce Coleman, Inc.*); **Bottom Right,** Hans Pfletschinger (*Peter Arnold, Inc.*)

Page Twenty-Two: Top, Eldon L. Reeves (*Tom Stack & Associates*); **Middle Left and Middle Right,** Kjell B. Sandved; **Bottom Left,** Dan Guravich (*Photo Researchers*); **Bottom Middle,** Kjell B. Sandved; **Bottom Right,** Anthony Bannister (*Natural History Photographic Agency*)

Page Twenty-Three: Top Left, L. West (*Bruce Coleman, Inc.*); **Top Right,** Prato (*Bruce Coleman, Ltd.*); **Middle,** Moldvay (*After Image*); **Bottom Right,** Med Beauregard (*PPS*)

Our Thanks To: David Faulkner (*San Diego Museum of Natural History*); James S. McElfresh (*SDSU*); Lynnette Wexo

Cover Photo: Lubber grasshopper

Contents

Insects are the most successful creatures on earth. Their bodies and behaviors have been adapted in different ways so that they can live almost everywhere, eat almost any food, and survive under almost any conditions.

Today, there are more than a million species of insects in the world. In terms of numbers, no other group of animals even comes close. There are only about 5,000 species of mammals.

Insects have been so remarkably successful because they are very efficient at finding food and mates, building shelters, communicating with each other, and sometimes even working together.

As you can imagine, with so many different kinds of insects, there is an almost endless variety of ways that they accomplish these things. In this book, you will see some of the most fascinating things that insects do. And you will learn how they help to make our world a better place to live.

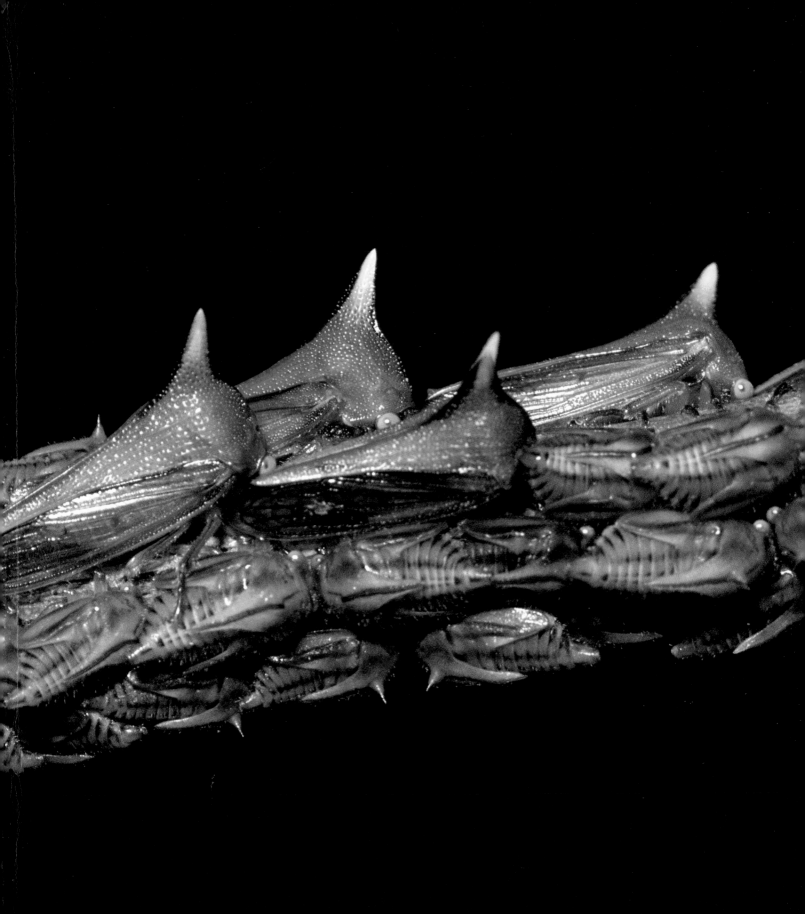

TREE HOPPERS
THORN DISGUISE

Many plants need bees and insects to carry pollen from flower to flower. If there were no insects to do this, there would be few flowering plants and no fruit.

BURYING BEETLE

When animals die, their bodies lie on the ground. If they weren't removed, they would just pile up. Many insects help to keep the world clean by eating dead animals.

ORCHARD CLOSED

HONEYBEE

You need insects more than you probably realize. Every day, in many ways, insects are doing things that make your life better. In fact, the whole world would be different if there were no insects. And your life would be different too.

If there were no insects, you would have fewer foods to eat. There would be no fruit and only a few vegetables. Many beautiful things would disappear from the world. Most birds would be gone, as well as many other animals. Few colorful flowers would grow. Without insects, the world would be dirtier, poorer, and more ugly.

On these pages, we show the world resting on the back of an ant. In a way, insects do hold up the world.

Every day, many trees and plants die and fall to the ground. If it weren't for insects, there would be piles of dead wood everywhere. Wood-boring insects often eat dead wood and drill holes in it. This helps bacteria enter and rot the wood. When the dead wood is removed, there is space for new trees to grow.

WOOD-BORING BEETLE

Insects are an important food supply for many spiders, reptiles, fish, birds, and mammals. If there were no insects to eat, most of these animals would die. And this would cause a severe food shortage for all other animals and people.

MOLE CRICKET

Plants can't grow in soil that is too tightly packed, because they can't spread their roots. Many insects and other small animals loosen the soil and make it possible for plants to grow. One of the best diggers is the mole cricket. If you look closely at its front legs, you'll see that they are built like little shovels.

Insects eat almost everything.

This is one reason for their great success. Most insects are plant eaters. In fact, there is an insect to eat practically every part of every plant in the world. Many live in the soil, where they feed on roots or decaying plant life. Some chew into stems and branches. Others eat leaves. And thousands of them eat nectar from flowers.

The larvae of insects usually eat more than the adults. Like children, their bodies are growing rapidly and they need more food. Often the larvae eat different foods than the adults. For example, the larvae of some species prey on other insects, but when they become adults they are plant eaters.

Flowers produce a liquid sugar called *nectar* to attract insects. When an insect goes into a flower to get the nectar, some pollen sticks to its body. Then the insect carries the pollen to other flowers.

DRAGONFLY

Dragonflies are expert fliers. They can even catch mosquitos, midges, and small moths in midair. With their enormous eyes, they can spot their prey from almost any angle. They bring their six bristly legs together like a trap to catch their prey.

SCALE INSECTS

Two of the most popular foods for insects are stems and leaves. Because insects concentrate on different parts of plants, there may be room for thousands of them to feed on a single plant at the same time. Some bite and chew the edges of leaves. Others devour the whole leaf. Scale insects, like those shown here, pierce the stem and suck out the liquid inside.

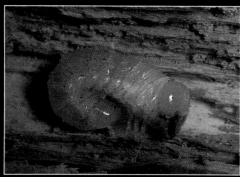

The larvae of bark beetles have an easy time finding food. They are born sitting on top of an endless supply of it. The female bark beetle deposits her eggs right in the bark of a tree. So when the larvae hatch, they are surrounded by wood. As with most insects, the larvae eat huge amounts. But strangely, most adult bark beetles do not eat any wood at all.

LARVA OF BARK BEETLE

There are even insects that catch fish! Some giant waterbugs grow to be four inches long and can catch fish twice their size. They use their powerful forelegs to grab their prey.

When the praying mantis hunts, it lo as though it is praying. And this is ho got its name. The mantis stands perfe still with its sharp forelegs held toget It may wait in this position for hours u an insect comes within reach. Then, s denly, it leaps forward with lightn speed and snares the insect.

Many plants have developed defenses to keep insects from eating their seeds. Some seeds have very hard covers. But some insects have ways to break through these covers. This weevil has a long, hard snout that can cut right into the hard shell of an acorn.

food and mates, and to escape from animals that would like to eat them. Because the bodies of insects are so small, there isn't much space for sense organs. For this reason, some sense organs may be located in strange places. And some insects combine several senses in one organ.

For example, some parts of an insect's antennae may be used to hear. But other parts may be used to touch, smell, or taste. Some insects use the hairs on their legs and feet to feel. But they may also use other hairs in the same area to smell and taste. Hairs may even sense such things as warmth, or dampness, or how hard the wind is blowing!

This insect has thousands of hairs all over its body. And it can use many of them to feel and smell. Imagine what it would be like having thousands of fingers and noses all over your body!

Many insects have eyes that are much different from yours. Each of your eyes has a single lens that can see one image at a time. But the eyes of most insects can have thousands of lenses, and can see thousands of images at the same time. This kind of eye is called a *compound eye.* Because each of the lenses in a compound eye points in a slightly different direction, an insect can see in many directions all at once. This fly can see in 12,000 directions at the same time!

ROBBER FLY

EYE OF FRUIT FLY

Some flies can do more than see with their compound eyes. They can also use them to *feel.* The tiny hairs between the lenses of this eye are feelers.

Some insects that eat nectar use their feet to taste it. They brush the bottom of their feet over the surface of a flower to see if any nectar is there. If they find some, they start eating it immediately. As they eat, their feet continue to look for more. How would you like to be able to taste sugar with your feet?

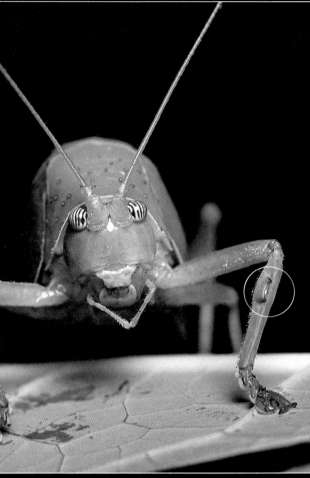

The long, fuzzy things on this moth's head look like antennae. But they're not. They are tasters called *sensory palps*. This moth brushes its palps over plants to see if it can taste anything that might be good to eat.

The antennae of insects have different shapes because they are used for different purposes. Many moths have long, feathery antennae to pick up smells in the air. The spoon-shaped antennae on the beetle below are used for tracking ants. The ants leave a scent trail as they walk. And the antennae are sensitive enough to smell it.

Katydids have their ears on their legs! It is important for them to hear well, because the females find their mates by listening for the sounds that the males make. By changing the positions of their legs, the katydids can listen for sounds from any direction. Just think, if you had ears on your legs, you could turn them in many different directions too.

The longhorn beetle has the longest antennae of any insect in the world. The antennae can be *three times longer* than the rest of its body. One of these beetles actually had antennae that were 10½ inches long!

Insects communicate in many different ways. They send signals that other insects can see, hear, smell, feel, or taste. Some of these signals are warnings meant to keep other insects from attacking them. These signals are easily recognized by other species.

But many messages are meant only for members of the same species. They are sent in secret codes that outsiders cannot understand. Insects send these secret messages by tapping, flashing, stroking each other, releasing chemical odors, or even "singing and dancing."

Most of these codes are used to locate a mate. But they may be used for a number of other purposes as well. For example, they may alert other insects to approaching danger or tell them where to find food.

Many female moths send out chemical signals to attract a mate. When they release even a tiny amount of their "perfume" into the air, males will pick up the scent and come flying. See if you can follow the scent that this female moth is sending out.

MALE HOUSE CRICKET

Male crickets "chirp" to attract females. They produce this musical sound by making the inside edges of their front wings vibrate. To do this, they rub their wings together, just like a violin bow rubs the strings.

Honeybees use dances to tell other bees where nectar is located. A bee that finds nectar performs a dance when she returns to the hive. The *round dance* (shown below) tells the other bees there is food within 110 yards. The dancing bee runs around in a circle, then turns and repeats the dance in the opposite direction.

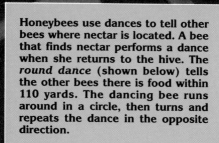

PERIODICAL CICADA

A male cicada can make the loudest sound of any insect. It produces the sound by vibrating a pair of "drums" located on the sides of its abdomen. The shrill "music" of one cicada can be heard more than a quarter of a mile away.

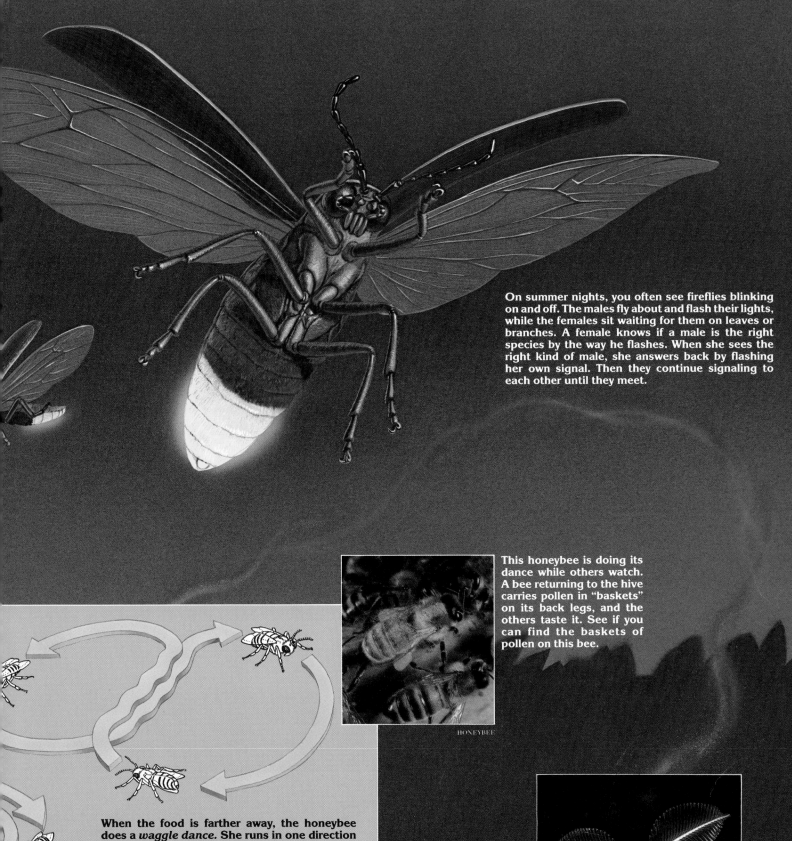

On summer nights, you often see fireflies blinking on and off. The males fly about and flash their lights, while the females sit waiting for them on leaves or branches. A female knows if a male is the right species by the way he flashes. When she sees the right kind of male, she answers back by flashing her own signal. Then they continue signaling to each other until they meet.

This honeybee is doing its dance while others watch. A bee returning to the hive carries pollen in "baskets" on its back legs, and the others taste it. See if you can find the baskets of pollen on this bee.

HONEYBEE

When the food is farther away, the honeybee does a *waggle dance.* She runs in one direction while waggling her body from side to side. Then she returns to her starting point and repeats the waggle. The direction of the waggling line tells the other bees what direction to fly. And they know how far to fly by how rapidly she waggles and the number of waggles she makes.

Giant silk moth males may have the best sense of smell in the world. With their huge antennae, they can smell a tiny amount of a female's perfume from nearly *seven miles* away!

MALE PROMETHEUS MOTH

17

Social insects are different from other insects because they live together in groups that can be very large. These groups are called *colonies*, and they may contain thousands and thousands of insects. Termites and ants, as well as some bees and a few wasps, live in large colonies.

All social insects have at least three things in common. The adults cooperate in *caring for the young*. Different members of the group are responsible for *different jobs*. And in each group there is at least *one queen*.

A queen produces all the young, and she may live many times longer than the other members of the group. She also sends chemical messages that may control the actions of the others. Her messages are passed from one member to the next throughout the colony.

The members of termite colonies have different bodies for different jobs. The large termite above with the huge head is a soldier. It is big and powerful, so it can defend the colony. The smaller termites are workers. There are more workers in a colony than anything else. They gather food, build and repair the nest, and tend the eggs. Some termites have wings and can fly. A few of these may become queens.

ARMY ANTS

Social insects are highly organized for finding food. Army ants probably have the most complex organization of all. They march in huge troops, sometimes over a million strong. Traveling at incredible speeds, they devour whatever lies in their path. The army ants shown above are carrying away a wasp nest for food.

FORMICA ANTS

Some ants are "farmers." They raise "herds" of aphids and "milk" them for honeydew. The ants protect their herds from predators. And they get aphids to release the honeydew by stroking them with their antennae.

SOLDIER TERMITES

Some soldier termites have huge jaws that they can use for crushing intruders. By smelling other insects, they can tell whether or not they are strangers. If they are, the soldiers immediately attack them.

Honeybee colonies are different from those of termites and ants. Worker bees do *all* the different jobs that need to be done. In its short life, every worker progresses from one job to another job. It starts as a house cleaner and ends as a food gatherer. In this box, we show the major stages in the life of a worker bee.

Every worker bee is born from an egg laid by the queen. She deposits one small egg in each perfectly shaped cell of the honeycomb. Three days later, a larva hatches. When the larva is ready to begin changing into an adult, its cell is sealed shut with white wax, like the one shown at left.

HONEYBEE QUEEN

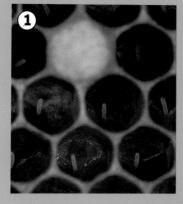

It takes 21 days for the larva to become an adult. Then it emerges from its cell, ready to go to work.

There can only be one queen bee in a hive. She is fed and cleaned by the workers, so that she can spend all of her time laying eggs. The workers make pollen into a special *royal jelly*, which they feed to the queen. This helps her lay up to 2,000 eggs per day.

When a worker bee comes out of its cell, it spends the first three days of adult life as a "house cleaner." Then it becomes a nurse, feeding and caring for the larvae.

After spending about one week as a nurse, the worker takes on new jobs. It may build new honeycombs or become a soldier to guard the entrance of the hive. Like soldier termites, the bees can identify intruders by their smell and attack them.

Worker bees have short lives. In summer they only live four to five weeks. For the last few weeks, they spend their time searching for nectar and pollen. Most of the food that they find is brought back to the hive and given to the nurses for storage.

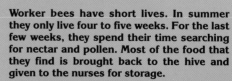

Insects build a great variety of structures for many reasons. These may be very simple, or very complex. Some of them build little "houses" that are barely large enough for themselves or their young. But social insects often build elaborate "cities" that may hold hundreds of thousands of insects.

Many adult insects protect their eggs with special structures. And often, larvae will construct their own shelters to keep them safe while they develop into adults.

CUCKOO SPITTLE BUG

WOODNYMPH BUTTERFLY

The larvae of some moths and butterflies spin beautiful silk cocoons. A cocoon gives protection to the young insect while it is developing into an adult. The cocoon shown here is unusual because it is made of only a few strands of silk.

LACEWING

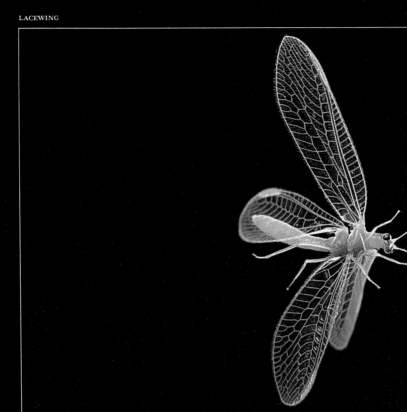

WEAVER ANTS

Many insects use plants to shelter their eggs. The lacewing uses a leaf as a roof over its eggs. It hangs rows of long rods from the leaf and then lays its eggs on the ends of the rods, as shown at right.

These tropical ants use silk in a different way. To make a nest, they pull leaves together and fasten them with silk. Often, the ants must build living bridges to reach from one leaf to another, as shown above.

CADDIS FLY LARVA

A caddis fly larva makes a suit of armor to live in. It builds a tough, protective tube out of twigs, leaves, shells, and anything else it can find.

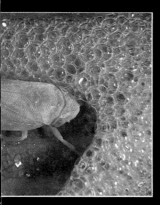

The spittle bug builds a house of bubbles! It blows the bubbles from plant juices. Some spittle bugs surround themselves with masses of bubbles many times larger than they are. This helps protect them because predators usually don't look for food in a big pile of bubbles.

INSIDE TERMITE MOUND

Some African termites live in skyscrapers. They build mounds over *40 feet high.* To do this, they stick billions of grains of sand together with their saliva. Inside one of these mounds, there may be hundreds of miles of tunnels.

POTTER WASP

EGGS OF LACEWING

A female potter wasp makes a little clay pot for a nest. She uses her front legs to make little balls of clay. Then she puts them together to build a pot. Once she lays her egg inside the pot, she makes a cover and closes it.

People and insects have been fighting each other for centuries. We have been battling with some insects because they eat food that we want to eat. And we want to get rid of others because they carry diseases. But no matter how hard we fight them, we don't seem able to win. In fact, destructive insects are a bigger problem for people today than they have ever been before.

Often the methods we use to control insects don't work. And some of the chemicals we use may even be dangerous to people. But scientists have been trying to find better ways to control insects. If these methods are successful, the way we look at insects may change in the future. Instead of competing with us for food, some insects may help us to have more food.

WASP COCOONS ON CATERPILLAR

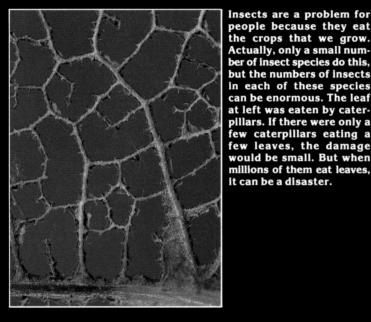

Insects are a problem for people because they eat the crops that we grow. Actually, only a small number of insect species do this, but the numbers of insects in each of these species can be enormous. The leaf at left was eaten by caterpillars. If there were only a few caterpillars eating a few leaves, the damage would be small. But when millions of them eat leaves, it can be a disaster.

BOLL WEEVIL

LADYBUGS

People have caused many of the problems that we have with insects by planting huge fields of crops. This is the cheapest way to raise food and other crops. But it also concentrates great numbers of plants in one place, and draws insects by the millions. For example, when people plant huge fields of cotton, this is an invitation to millions of boll weevils to come to a feast.

Most of the time, people try to control insects by spraying poisons called *insecticides* in huge quantities. This not only kills destructive insects, but helpful insects as well. And it may end up harming people too. In most cases, chemicals are *not* the best way to control insects.

For thousands of years, some insects have been providing food and other useful products to people. For example, the caterpillars of silk moths have been making silk. And bees have been giving us honey. Today, we are learning how to get more useful things from insects. For instance, farmers are finding new ways to use bees and other insects to help pollinate their plants. And some scientists think that insects may be a source for new chemicals and medicines.

In many cases there are better solutions to the insect problem than insecticides. Scientists are finding ways to use some insects to destroy other insects that damage our crops. For example, ladybugs like to eat aphids and scale insects. We can breed ladybugs and use them to control these pests. Robber flies prey on a wide variety of destructive insects. And the larvae of chalcid wasps can be used to destroy caterpillars as shown above. The adult wasp lays its eggs on a caterpillar, and as the larvae grow they eat the caterpillar.

Robber flies are often killed by insecticides. When we don't spray, the flies can help us to control other insects naturally.

Insects are high in protein. For this reason, they are already used for food in some parts of the world. In the future, as the world population continues to grow, it will get harder and harder to feed everybody. And insects may become a vital food source for us all. For example, insects may be made into flour and used to make bread.

Index